About Time, Too

by

Vivien Jones

Indigo Dreams Publishing

First Edition: Vivien Jones

First published in Great Britain in 2010 by:
Indigo Dreams Publishing
132 Hinckley Road
Stoney Stanton
Leics
LE9 4LN

www.indigodreams.co.uk

Vivien Jones has asserted her right under the Copyright, Designs and Patents Act 1988 to be identified as the author of this work.
©2010 Vivien Jones

ISBN 978-1-907401-25-1

British Library Cataloguing in Publication Data. A CIP record for this book can be obtained from the British Library.

Designed and typeset in Palatino Linotype by Indigo Dreams.

Cover design by Vivien Jones.

Printed and bound in Great Britain by Imprint Academic, Exeter.

ACKNOWLEDGEMENTS

Some poems in this collection have been previously published in Boyne Berries, The Eildon Tree, Ginosko (USA), The Glasgow Review, Obsessed with Pipework, Magma, Markings, new*leaf* (Germany), Not A Muse (Haven Books. Hong Kong) Poetry Scotland, Pushing Out the Boat, Salt Horizon and Stripe (Templar Poetry).

I would like to thank all the people who have encouraged me in this writing lark – family, friends and fellow writers – who probably are unaware of how much they helped the enterprise.

CONTENTS

About Time, Too

Strange Flesh

I spied a grey log
beached
on a grey pebble shore.

Coming near,
a glint of bone showed
it was not a log.
A glint of bone showing
through a scoop in flesh,
made crosses, a spine.

A jaw with broken lines
of thin teeth,
gums stabbed away
by complaining gulls,
no fins, no tail, no eyes,
no name.

A sea creature wrecked
by a violent tide,
a dry rotting banquet on
hot stones.
Because it is nameless,
small boy like, I take a stick
to punish its leather carcase.

Shore Voices

Estuary water sometimes glides
without waves over pebbles
that chuckle in the backwash.

Other times, wind makes waves
hiss as they piggyback to shore.
disintegrating into spinning foam.

An ecstatic dog flies through
a cold paw-deep tide, barking
its inexpressible joy to the water.

Tribes of birds that float make
soft rafts, islands of down and cackle,
safe on the lilting sea.

Midnight, moon and mountains
make a film star of the sea,
whispering intoxicating sounds.

I, intoxicated, sing to the waves.
Much of me is water, I'm told,
The best part, sings the sea.

Verses For The 79 Bus (Carlisle To Dumfries)

I

Elvis, 69, with stick
and babe, (not much younger)
get on.

'Where to ?'
'Cairndale Hotel'
'Sure it's no Heartbreak ?'

Invisible from the front,
hearing aid nestled,
grey-pink plastic
behind her ear.
Fine henna strands of hair,
whirled like meringue.
From behind, she is 19,
except for the hearing aid.

Passengers crane to look.
Elvis ignores them,
Crinkled black boot polish hair,
stiff enough to bear anything
bar a direct overhead hit.
Jeans, suede crepes,
Waxy soles
black studded leather jacket
rings on his fingers

He scans their greyness
No bothered.

She wriggles,
even sitting down,
she wriggles.
Satin dirndl skirt,
socks and pumps,
wrong earrings,
Bit 60s, those.
They whisper tenderly.

Huddled like beans,
Beloved old clothes
on their backs
modestly bristling with style,
The King and Priscilla
off to Dumfries.

II

What now?
Why is George (autistic)
Rolling his head back
howling with delight ?
Seen a rainbow,
Whole one,
Whole bloody one,
One foot in New Abbey,

The other in Ruthwell.
Dan (Downs Syndrome)
Sees it too,
smiles.
We (normal) look away
Don't meet his eye,
whatever you do.
You might have to admit
 rainbows make you smile too.
(learning difficulties – me?)

III

Lads in the back
Fuckety, fuck, fuck
Aye he did !
Get off, he's no that hard !
Wi one hand!

Girl gets on.
Clacks on sling-backs,
t-shirt two sizes too tight,
breasts on the stunning move.
Football cheers,
boys being men.
She's game.
Stands there, on show.
She smiles.
Silence.

Blushing among the plukes,
Fuckety, fuck, fuck
She smiles.
Takes her seat.

IV

She's met a pal.
Mobiles tingling,
Britney and Mozart.
Mozart?
'My mother bought it.'
Their swirling topknots
bob as they chat
'And did ye?'
'Aye.'
'Are ye seein him again?'
'Na.'
'How no?'
'I'm saving up,
Goin to Ibiza.
In June.'
'Been there.'
'Was it good?'
'A'right.'
'Thought I'd go before I get married.'
'Married?'
'Aye, next year'
'Who to?'
'Don't know yet.'

Saw Mill
Creca

We took three lengths of beech,
Leg-length long, arm-length diameter,
grey skin, barked in satin,
white wood showing,
we end-over-ended them
towards the bedlam shed.

The men and the blades
danced over the wood,
the back and forwards bed
fed the cylindrical lengths
to the spinning blade;
the blade spat boards, just so.

Curve and knot and ripple,
rolling out from the saw
emerge now, even slices;
the men gesture, all speech
swallowed by the mill roaring
at its workload; a screech,

the quick spark of a severed nail,
a saw blade's life shortened.
The men wipe their brows, frown,
over a calculation more troubling.
How much to turn a graceful tree
to usefulness –to squares, to blocks ?

Log Pattern Quilt. C 1900.

This tells my life, this quilt,
this sequence of incident in
stitches as numerous as the tears
shed for each lack, each loss.
The colours tell a true tale,
brief greens of spring and summer growth,
the splash of the blazing blue stream
gives way to longer dry harvest gold
and the dull grey slabs of winter.

In the middle is the non-colour
where Jamie died, I stitching
all through the dull days of waiting.
Those red circles are not flowers
but record the spray of his red breath.
Three summers old when we buried him
beside his sister, not yet one year.
My forefinger is dented with the
blunt press of the needle,
felt, not seen, in the faint autumn light
as the quilt grows across my knee
and the pile of infant clothes
grows smaller by my feet.

Museum Of Rural Life
Kiltimagh, Ireland April 2008

If you stand just here
And stare across there,
you can just see the print
of a house, very small,
on the hillside.

The woman who lived there,
if she stared across here,
could see this glass
and concrete building,
and wonder what it was.

More amazing than that,
if she saw inside it
and saw that her kitchen
tools were there, roped off,
labelled, forbidden, clean.

She might be puzzled,
if she thought about it,
that so many people
would stare for so long
at things so commonplace.

Chambers Street Museum.
Edinburgh

Once there were two boys
who whooped with joy
discovering
a horseshoe staircase,
the endless potential of gaining
the upper landing while I stood
perplexed at the bottom.
The younger one, still a toddler,
cried out in giddy triumph.
 "Toobla! Toobla!"
(his word for *toothbrush* and
many other secret things)

The older one, eyes sparkling, shouted
"Which way ? Which way, Mum?"

Nothing in that palace of mysteries
exceeded this joy.
Not the small birds,
impaled in frozen flight
like model aeroplanes,
Nor the black industrial dinosaurs,
or the glass-eyed stuffed ones,
whatever their majesty of scale,
caused my sons to glow so.

Their laughter flying across
that vast air space
caused a convergence of keepers.
"Shhhhh!" they chorused,
as if life itself could be silenced.

'Gardeners' Question Time' At Polmaddy *

'Maisie Barbour farmhand and herbalist'

'So, what can you recommend for a raw Galloway hillside
upon which an abandoned settlement sinks in its own echoes ?

A whaleback horizon, black at dusk, guiding soft constant rainfall
onto earth pocked with rocks and fibrous grasses tough enough
to capture soil in plaited roots, our own shit for manure.

We plant in rigs, sharing the sweet west lie, only the toughest
crops will throw themselves skywards, defying the slashing wind,
onions, small as marbles, cooked whole, make pungent soup.

I gather the healing plants, for bitter gruels and poultices,
called to wounds and vomitings, my wealth in my apron folds,
I keep them from the earth with the fruit of the earth.

The children dig granite stones, stacked in cairns with which
we build an inn, we stop the pilgrims in their path to Whithorn,
faith makes them thirsty, we are rich, we have many buildings.

No more, one summer they brought the sheep and we, like sheep,
were herded away to the barren towns.
Will you make a garden here where once the stripe of the rigs told
where the fruitful earth lay ?'

Polmaddy is the site of an 18th century 'ferme-toun' almost lost among the tough grasses of the Galloway countryside.

Churching Hat. 1894. Parton.

Mother opened the cardboard box
and I beheld my churching hat.

Such soft bewitching browns, the brown of fur,
some creature's coat wrapped round the rim
to warm my Sunday neck in Parton Church.
The stroking brown of velvet, warm on the hand,
pocked with spotted leaves and skin tones,
rosied into a flower above my forehead.
a swirl of weightless brown feather on top.
My ignorant open-eyed question ;
'Are ostriches brown, Mother ? And do tell me,
 where, near to Parton, are there ostriches ?'

With trembling hands I set the V at the nape
over my knotted hair; I pull the speckled bronze
net over my face.
Mother looked at me through the gauze,
she sighed.
'You're all grown up now,' she said,
so sadly.

Hare

It was a sloping field
tipped towards the sea,
the breeze blew
along the ground,
cooling my bare legs.

My foot was nearly down,
poised at the point where
weight shifts forward.
I may have heard
its indrawn breath
before
its silk gloved paws
glanced off my leg.
Erupting through
the tussocks, it shrank
to rabbit, then mouse.

Through the fence,
into the sea mist,
making a story
for telling to children.

Earthbound
Traquair Fair

A summer festival,
behind the raucous arena
amongst the ruffling hawks
and volatile falcons,
a raven, black all over,
wild eyed and shackled,
stretches a parallel leg and wing.

I see the sheared primaries,
watch him lift his head
towards the howling peacock
blacked-out in the branches above,
side-on, sharp as a paper cut,
tail trailing, a drag anchor,
princess crown bobbing.

A cool breeze trembles the birds,
the raven tilts his silken head.
opens his gawping jaw,
launches his ratchet croak to a sky
that he is forbidden.
The peacock stirs, glides to earth
in a parody of flight, a taunting lie.
The raven turns his back, hops away.

The air is thick with sparrows.

Walking with Bosch

Foot and Mouth, Spring 2001
after a calming interval

I

Usually, I walk to my bus
up the gentle curve of the hill
my back to the sea,
forever turning round to
examine its glittering advances.
In the browsed fields
some inexact number of
sheep and cows graze.
Jackdaws, lapwings and gulls
toss themselves into the air,
quarrelling.
Nearly every day
there will be a weasel undulating
frantically across my path,
or an electric vole in spasm,
and always, buzzards mewing
across an open sky

Across the water, Cumbria farms lie
under a playful, streaking mist,
Skiddaw, head up, basks in its own
precipitate sunlight.

At Great Orton, the windmills bat
silver light back at the sun.
From this rose-tinted distance
landscape is both fresh forged
and ancient.

II

One Tuesday, things are different.
The fields with their ragwort dregs
have emptied.
There are mud tracks at the entrance
and notices flutter on the gates
like gulls pinned by the wing.
By the gate-post a sawn-off plastic can
offers a disinfectant ritual
for a new sacrament.
On the hill the smoke starts,
cooking beef turns to burning beef,
choking hair and bone smoke,
reeking, reeking.
The sheep and their pipe-cleaner lambs
have disappeared.
I walk with Bosch,
with pestilence and burning.
The windmills across the water,
Mark a sacrificial burial place,
and many fields fly a plume
of orange hearted smoke.
The plague markers are on the gates,

red capitals, keep out.
On my walk I meet the farmer.
He shakes his head, shrugs,
folds his arms, scratches his head.
'Oh well,' he says, disintegrating.

III

Once again, I walk to the bus
up the gentle curve of the hill.
This mild winter has healed the fields
with flushes of new grass
and lemon gorse flowers.
Today, there were thirty four sheep
and eighteen cows in the fields,
wandering amongst rabbits that
had appropriated the empty fields.
They have no folk-lore, no historian.
They do not know that the woman
who paused to count the sheep
is not in search of sleep but
suffers a persistent smell in the memory.

Code Of Practice

(It is illegal to use a tape recording to attract geese for shooting)

Vapours thread through the reeds,
sun poking blue holes in the mist,
the croaking of squabbling ducks
shouted down by a thumping bass
persuading the waking geese to boogie.

*(shooting geese leaving their roosts in the morning causes less
disturbance than shooting them when they return in the evening)*

Not quite awake then,
not really minding the blaze in the breast,
a neighbour tumbling down, broken winged,
the rest of the day to survive,
before a very final rest.

*(the shooting of ducks and geese in Scotland on a Sunday is
prohibited)*

God loves geese- but do they know,
that once in every seventh sunrise
they might cease watching for
Barbour hats and mad spaniels,
for men, too, must love geese on Sundays.

Considering *An Gorta Mór*

Is this really a day out – this grey shore,
this grey sea merged with this grey sky
beneath this grey hillside, *Cruach Phádraig.*

The tea room is shut, the church ruins are damp
and nettle strewn, the walls streaming,
topped by birds in red stockings, the choughs.

A ship on stones, more whole than many that sailed,
interlaced with skeletons, pointing away,
there are no words, no feeling enough.

I take a photo, capturing nothing of my thoughts
on men who took money from a people uncounted
 in their *scalps**, who may have been one million.

*Scalps : a hole in the earth covered with twigs and turf.
The families who lived in them were not counted in the
1841 census.

Hardware Shop

He's playing the crowd,
he's charming, he knows it.
The cameras flash on him,
his cat in the window,
curved in sleep on a box,
is well practiced too.
So many small drawers
with small things
in many sizes,
as few as you want
in a newspaper twist.
Rat-traps on a string
spiralling to the roof,
beside the wooden stair
that led to the upstairs bar,
one of many in the street.

So we gaze but do not buy,
We have no skill that
needs his precise stock,
measured in imperial.
Today he has sold a mousetrap
and a bottle of white spirit,
to a local woman who stood
aside while we took his picture.

Next year, like as not,
his door, too, will be shut,
soon to be a branch
of something from Dublin,
People will say Shame,
and tell their grandchildren
about the Hardware shop
that used to sell nails
in ones and twos,
and had a cat that dozed
in a curl on a cardboard box
in the window.

Kiltimagh Homestead
Kiltimagh,Ireland April 2008

These builders -they're gallus -
to throw up gorse yellow houses
straight off the pattern pages,
four pillars or six, all the same,
in sight of the old place

with its creeping damp,
its rotten tooth boundaries,
iron roof still corrugated,
perforated with rust aertex,
stones now green from grey.

But for all the stripe of the lawns,
the curve of Spanish arches,
a water feature trickling over
copper bowls, solar lights
that curve towards the house,

there is gorse scratching
at the stucco garden wall
to get in amongst the flowers,
thorns beneath a coconut cloud,
flowers not for picking.

On the hillside beyond,
gorse shows its tenacity,
a horseshoe of flame
scorched to the root,
and it's dead

for a while.

Cell
Kiltimagh 2008

It's Spring but there are no leaves yet.
Rather, silver-streaked birches
stencil black sprays of hairline twigs
against a sky emptied of blue by cold.
They grow near and through the boulders
of the wall, a painful stack of labour
outlining a place cleared for burial.

Graves as ordered as Christians in church,
face east for the last sunrise.
An ivy-strangled oak throws shadows,
across the roof of the guardian cell,
its snakeskin stonework slippery
with the residue of daily mists,
its cold interior leaching faith from
the body of its visitors
as it once did its monks.

Better the cutting wind, the frozen light,
the company of the dead outside
than the dank gloom of stone and doubt inside.

Higher English
Kirkwall 2008

On the school desk I arrange my notes,
my books, my stimulus cards, over and over.
The clock closes on the wedge of two pm,
a shocking bell-buzzer rips the air,
my mouth and mind are dry and empty.
The room is suddenly filled with lovely
young women and men, lounging, examining.

I am introduced - generously.

I have chosen Duffy for her empathy
with teenage pain and passion – I know my text
but muddle my intro; do they realise this
falls straight into their Reflective Writing file,
that it will deliver them the possibility of writing
an analytical essay of some quality ?
The lovely young women and men shift in their seats.

They want more.

I hand them the pictures; they take up their pencils.
I tell them about those rare lessons
when words, potent as any cocktail
first stirred and shook me, not to write
essays but to run through the woods
shouting bright words, to weep onto my diary,
to look with my own eyes at my world.

Do that – I say – do that.

At last, they smile.

Boarding Now
1C Bus – Stromness to Kirkwall

From harbour to harbour,
this bus noses along slim roads,
snaking between treeless hills,
its company loudly sharing news
of people not on the bus;
a cast list of first names.

I am the stranger here among
rows of wind lined Viking faces,
the women small and strong,
the men long limbed and wiry.
At the sound of my voice
they turn as one to measure my presence.

November, so maybe no tourist,
Mid-morning, so no worker,
English, but no BBC radio accent,
Female, so not Enterprise,
Bright clothes, so no ornithologist,
Alone with a bus pass, so no lover.

Sea-sensible imaginations stir.
I may be a mystic returning
to stoke up old fires, thaw the blood
of sleeping warriors who ride this bus
whilst a sea-going ship is taking shape
in the wild waters off Brough Head.

At the harbour edge this company
rise as one, baskets like shields,
babies on backs, a tribe set for foraging
among the stone buildings and wynds,
whilst I, only a little poetic, drink coffee
in the jazz café trying to regain reason..

Flight
Glasgow to Orkney - October 2008

I am alone at the airport.
I drink more coffee than I want.
A 'real' pasty, microwaved,
warm on the brown outside,
with scalding grey innards,
cloys in my mouth.
Watching the minute hand
strain against gravity,
another last trip
to the fragrant Ladies.
I crocodile with the others,
cross the tarmac to the plane.
Bodywork thinner than our car,
entry by step-ladder,
propellers.
Fight or flight?
I can't turn back, I'm being paid.

On its thin legs, the plane
trundles to the runway,
rears, roars into the blue,
I read my book so no-one
sees my fear, drink orange
when it banks northwards,
look and see Google Earth
below, a smooth scrolling
of maps, physical, in geography,

all the browns and greens
in the world, crowned in snow,
laced with water.

By Orkney I have crossed
more than miles,
I leave the plane in smiles.

Dining with Copernicus
'Al Brindisi', Ferrara

Piercing the shadows of narrow alleys,
the dusk sun sneaks a low beam
onto a sign board – *Al Brindisi AD 1435* -
yet another 'oldest tavern in Europe.'

Banquettes, dark wine bottles
behind chicken wire frames,
a wooden board with cheese
spiralled from mild to ferocious,
the waiters whisper and offer
only expensive wine.

My place mat, made of brown paper,
says that Tasso and Cellini ate here,
so did the student Copernicus,
who, seeing this same sky,
thought up earth moving heresies.

So do I, walking slowly back,
seeing the full moon through
the open oval above a courtyard,
thinking of the curious Copernicus,
a moment's dizziness may just
have been the angle of my gaze,
but it felt like the moon sucking.

Pisa, as in *Leaning Tower of....*

Pizza at midnight in a lamplit square,
we saw nothing on our white taxi ride
through a city smeared by drizzle.
Our companions an old man, mother, infant,
the quiet curl of a dog at their feet,
our waiter waits forever.

In Geography every place on earth was
sunlit, every country bright coloured
with parakeet people, every city boasted
its signature building, except ours.

Pacing the pages of textbooks,
straight for the heart of the city,
catching white wedding cake flashes
through gaps in office blocks ;
we hurry, we centre on our target,
and it's there, it's there.

How could we know in that stunned moment
when geography books proved true,
that, next day, we would stare in Bologna
at a tower more skewed, less famous,
and think of Pisa as a bit of a strumpet,
smug that we bought no glass leaning tower.

Haiku After Florence

Thick dark chocolate,
roof-top of the Uffizi,
a sparrow underfoot

Haiku After Ferrara

Perfect miniature,
a town with oval sky views,
the moon falling through.

Haiku After Bologna

Blazing white jackets,
interrogator's lighting,
top dog restaurant.

The Sea So Close
Venice 2006

The sea, you know it,
waves and breakers,
pebbles and sand,
a clear boundary between.

Cool and paddlesome,
a crust of salt on
seaweed, limpets and
mussels for ornament.

But here;
my foot rests on land
licked by salt ripples,
some slow tide moves,

without fuss, over the path.
The sea climbs the buildings,
curved bridges wear barnacles
high on their sides.

I am walking on water.

Verses For The 82 (Water) Bus

(Valloresso to Ferrovia, Grand Canal, Venice)

A two man operation,
pilot and rope man.
One shapes the vessel's passage
through criss-cross traffic,
the other forms loose hoops
with his rope,
ready with a flourish
to toss a single loop
over the pier capstan,
whereupon,
instantly,
he pens a calligraphic flourish
of rope around the boat's capstan,
marrying one to the other.
The pilot guns into reverse,
water churns,
the knot slides tight,
passengers brace
for the hipping of boat and pier,
then trip off-board.

The boat draws back,
the rope man shakes his knot-work
loose on the deck.
A tourist records a commonplace skill,
a digital gasp to share, once home.

Pilot, rope man
and boat dance on,
next stop, the Rialto.

Chiesa di S.Giorgio Maggiore
Venice 2006

Ten euros for the tower.
We are hot already, unlikely
to enjoy the climb, stopping
for longer rests at shorter intervals,
just to hunt down that view.
We weigh up the discomfort.

You shrug, I succumb,
we walk towards the stairs,
to face a netting wall.
A robed and tonsured monk
approaches, motions us
towards a gleaming lift.

Long forbidden, long sloping
steps with shallow drops
encircle the lift shaft,
its steel skeleton humming.
We watch the stairs recede,
the monk smiles, speechless.

A swirl of wind balloons my skirt,
we lean out of our brick basket
blinded by sun on white buildings
and water, light that trembles
flashes evidence of glass on boats.
Water buses like fat woodlice interlace

with speedboats darting between
in joyful, suicidal transits,
a liner at rest, a Gulliver sleeping,
disturbs the scale of boats, buildings
and the grandest of canals, wearing
its gondolas, a plague of stick insects.

The monk is patient, speechless,
waiting for us to tire of the world,
seen as half-map, half-model below.
I raise my camera, catch a habitual
impatience cross his face; he knows
and I know the futility of possession.

Something In The Blood
After 'Great Silkie' 2005

I know he has been nowhere
but inside my body, this babe
who lies in sea anemone motion,
expressing the oceans
of his heredity.

My meek sea empathy
has been to paddle and swim some,
once in deep rough water
with salt smacks in my face,
close to surrender.

So it must be that sea genes
swam from my blood to his,
changing cells that were me
to not me, building a stranger
inside his skin.

We stare into the pool,
at refractions, reflections,
The image seem clear
but underneath, his otherness
stirs small fears.

Belated

Dear Frances, dear sister,
These are the things I never said
from when we were so jealous-
you thrashing me with your loveliness
and me thrashing you with my intelligence.
I never saw skin like yours,
peach bloom and shade in the morning,
freshly washed, spotless. I longed
to stare and stare and absorb you.

"No-one will ever want you.
You'll have to marry a teacher,"
you sneered.

You vamped my quiet (and only) boyfriend.
He, prostrate with astonishment,
pecked at me with absent-minded kisses.
I ditched him and kept the next one a secret.

"How come you're three years older
than me, and I'm doing your homework?"
I sneered.

I stole your only un-laddered seamed stockings
and hid them in my schoolbag. I knew
you wanted them for your new high heels,
but you didn't deserve to be that much ahead.

You were half right.
I did marry a teacher and,
since you're not around,
he does want me.

In The Middle

I am the fulcrum,
in my middle years,
past and future in equilibrium,
taking a balanced view,
I overhear your memories,
two brothers, both past fifty,
boys again, boys always,
feathers and driftwood,
incoming tide, offshore breeze.
A boat is born, not built, not thought,
but dreamed into being,
bobbing bravely out to sea.

My memory blazes,
a pale girl in Malta,
upside down in the sun
on the ex-naval exercise bars,
a jeer: 'Pinky Pants!'
a boy's cruel face,
the gathering of classmates,
the birth of a nickname,
a lingering hurt.

My leather clad son,
at fourteen, frightening me,
hair and metal, seeking sex,
rock music and bikes.
Girls softening his edges.
One girl, creeping inside.
There he is, lying on the floor
crooning to his baby,
a sweet heavy metal lullaby.

I hold my 12 hour grandson,
Life itself hums in my arms,
in sea anemone motion.
I plan his future memories,
books I will cosily read to him,
cakes we will messily bake,
walks across that pebble beach
where I, the fulcrum, now stand.

Best Medicine

A phone call,
'Come and get me.....'

My first child,
turning to man.
Insect jacket,
leather plated,
worn with worn denim,
patched like acne.
Chains add bravado
to his precarious self.

Bumfluff mouth
yawning,
Eyes to the kitchen,
'Could do with a nibble.'

Those mother questions;
When did you last
Eat,
Wash,
Sleep?
Asked silently
in case he fled.

Sometimes,
the best expression of love
is two bacon rolls at midnight,
and no comment.

Sea Urchin
Malta 1957

Beware, she said,
watch where you walk,
that silver sand
under glassy water,
pure as a Disney cartoon,
is home to spiked beasts
with poison barbs.

I paced, my small feet
touching so lightly,
I hardly felt the piercing
but heard the snap
as the barb broke.
The black spines quivered
in my soft sole, I howled
and mother whispered,
just before her hug,
'I told you so.'

Prince of Wales Road, Sliema

In the marble hall a slow staircase,
stepping up to the first floor, our door
open most of the time for visitors
my mother hopes for, who never come
to Prince of Wales Road, Sliema.

Theresa, the maid, barefoot and fat,
sweeps the dust from her own feet
straight through the railings,
falling in golden motes like magic,
never reaching the tiled floor.

My summer sleeping space,
up the spiral stair, past the ledge
where mother stores dark blue
'Surf' boxes, saving for sundae
dishes, six box tops for one,

to where green lizards cross
the light switches, cool air
from the roof aerates the
rattan bed, fluttering the
butterfly pages of my books.

My brother keeps tadpoles
in the basin, beside the terrace
where the apricot tree pulses.
Tadpoles turn to spotted frogs,
my sister screams, my mother smiles.

In Prince of Wales Road, Sliema,
my mother burns her hands
on a Primus stove, my father
wraps them in lint so gently.
When he tells her off, she crys.

My History Of Curry

First time. Vesta in a box,
that only Daddy ate.
Two bags, rice and sauce,
rolling in boiling water.
(But rice is for pudding!)
We watched, sniffing.
Once, in the dark kitchen,
I licked his cold plate.

First love, first date,
Cinema, chocolates,
dinner in the evening
at the new Indian place.
He chose from the mysteries
on the menu, nothing hot.
Then sex, with spices still
haunting the mouth.

New bride, new recipe book,
Shelves full of curry powders,
Sultanas, apple, boiled eggs,
A misfire of flavours.
Two newly married couples,
entertaining in convivial ignorance.
courtesy of Schwartz, Pataks,
and Sharwood,

Today, my curry contains
lemon grass and root ginger,
fresh chillies and minted raita.
Puffed up, charred fresh naans,
lean back to back, cooling.
Though the house is aromatic,
in a moment of doubt, I recall
the shock of Daddy's cold Vesta.

Digital Love
For Louis

You ring *me*, a habit we both accept,
not taking turns or assuming unequal need.
Your ever-forgiving reminder that
the lost years are now found,
creased, ready to be ironed out
by our digital love.

Sparks strike the ether
If our jokes and metaphors energise the air
between Edinburgh and here
between London and here,
driving a clean spear between the dutiful calls
of other mothers and sons,
that's because, just like them,
we are not like them.

Who had a babe like mine?
What babe's eyes glittered like yours?
What babe ever watched the world so intently?
What two year old ever memorised satisfying numbers?
(your first declaration of independence)
I was astonished and humbled and proud.
I pushed the pram of a prodigy
and no-one else suspected.

What do we talk about so vividly?
Our conversation, plates in the air.

Underneath them
we talk silently of sharing, understanding,
empathy and of the rushes of warmth
and loss that knock us over now and then.
Wrapped in your words in the cold hallway,
sometimes I tremble or shiver,
not being able to touch you
and owing you love.

Sea Dog

My daddy was a ship's carpenter,
a man that began on wooden ships
with hand tools, edges razor fine,
handles patinated with use.
He called the floor 'the deck'.

My daddy was a fisherman, an early riser,
on the road by sunrise on his motorbike,
headed for the rocks and the sea bass.
My dream and joy to go with him.
He called upstairs 'topside'.

My daddy was a Royal Navy man,
browned and bleached in Maltese summers.
At home on great grey metal ships
that still had wooden fittings.
He called my mother 'Pudding'.

My daddy was a fish, a porpoise,
a diver and thrasher, agleam in the sea.
He coaxed me into bottomless water,
I swam, I swam and he laughed and laughed,
He called me his 'water-baby'.

My daddy was anxious inland, reeling
from unfamiliar rhythms, city-sick,
His smell was salt and tobacco;
his stories were sea shanties unsung,
He called the sea 'my love'.

Whole Fish

I do love the boneless
wonder of pleats of fillets,
the sou'wester yellow of
your fat smoked haddock
and the sideways faces of
your plaice,
but, see that *whole* fish -
That silvered creature,
with head and tail
and chiffon fins,
film on his body,
blood in his eye,
Go on, open his jaw
show me the wild thing
out of the sea,
that ate his fellows,
let me eat him.

The fishmonger grins,
hands flecked with silver scales,
he folds an octopus
back on itself
like a salt flower.

Unwanted Immigrant

1964, pitched up in Dunfermline,
a slide back down the ladder of time.
It is Sunday and Scotland is closed.
I am sixteen, torn away from
the gleaming white phoenix
that is Plymouth.

I work in Edinburgh, over the water.
I cross on the criss-cross railway bridge.
They are still spanning the Forth
with a bridge that reaches out from either side,
but does not yet touch.

First Hogmanay – Christmas high-jacked
The nip of Windolene, new rugs,
the rubble of black bun caking the mouth,
Songs I do not know – why do I sing of Aberdeen?
Whisky kisses, whisky hands, a slap,
a caution from an older woman,
'Don't fuss, hen. It's Hogmanay.'

Come on, I'm winching you, aren't I?
Course I love you, come on,
If you let me we'll get engaged,
put ourselves down for a house.
I'll get a suit, three piece job.
Come on, they say English girls are hot.

My babies, sons of Scotsmen,
roaring boys in technicolour Babygros,
Picture Puffins from Bauermeisters,
Water babies in the Commonwealth Pool,
We ride the hissing maroon buses
across the Spring and Autumn city,
stay clear at the summer Festival.

Americans hissing obscenities,
stone faces at Faslane as they lift
us, linked together, a bone necklace
of limbs feigning limpness.
'We fought a war for the likes of you –
hippy cow', I can't stop crying,
He looks like my dad, sounds like my dad.

My voice defects, I hear it borrow words
to make me kin, but friends laugh,
tack a bowler hat and briefcase
to my identity – even though I am Cornish
and working class – I belong nowhere,
like the bridge that didn't meet, I have
a foot on two banks, a gap in the middle,
a borrowed home, a sheared-off past.

Octopus In Galloway

Such a Spring Sunday! Light that clarifies,
almost magnifies the long view of river reeds
and trees across the holm.
Rising late, barefoot in the kitchen
thinking of something special for lunch.

There it lies, opaque and gelatinous, flowing
across the plate in a calligraphic curve.
An octopus entire.

Cook it? Our Japanese guest blinks
'So sorry, don't know how.'
Humiliation rises around us.

'Wait!'
She phones, chatters, hangs up, arms folded,
waiting in silent Japanese calm.
The phone rings, the fax burbles.
A stream of paper like fresh pasta unrolls
from its slit mouth, instructions in Japanese
on how to cook a whole octopus.

Inside an octopus is a transparent blade
that holds its body in shape. Minus stiffening,
the octopus follollops on the cutting board.
She slices thin rings rapidly,
tosses them into the blue smoking wok.

So, which is the more amazing?
The salty see-through sea creature,
or a shoal of digital pulses flowing
from Japan to help cook a whole octopus on
such a Spring Sunday in Galloway?

Fry Up

He waits, legs akimbo,
at the window table,
cradling the red plastic tomato
in huge hands.
A thin girl with plaited hair
in a faded yellow tabard
places knife, fork and napkin before him,
makes the salt & pepper prominent
on the chequered plastic cloth.
He nods; a medieval courtesy.

A white plate arrives, steaming.
A fried egg, satin skirt, sunny eyed,
nestles against two crinkled rashers
of salty, charcoal flecked bacon.
A sausage curves glossily round
a black flush of mushrooms which
rest on a ledge of fried bread.
A tomato, split asunder, sizzles.

He sniffs deeply, takes up his fork,
spears a sausage and bites.
Closes his eyes to intensify
the burst of flavour, dribble appears
at the corner of his chomping mouth.

Outside the window,
three slim hungry women,
onlookers at the bus stop,
sniff and salivate.

'Overweight,' observes one,
'Heart attack,' predicts another,
'Bliss,' sighs the third.

The Moon In The Pail

Aesop's fox was no fool,
but neither was the wolf.
When he looked into the bucket
and saw that pale shimmering cheese,
the colour of winter butter
under the cooling water,

maybe he thought, why not –
do I care if the fox escapes?
Don't I love the cloaking taste
of cheese as it crumbles in
my jaws, better than a stringy
fox leg, even his rump meat
could not approach the rapture
of cheese flowing down my throat.

By the still pool
fringed and sheltered by tall reeds,
I kneel in the darkness,
scanning its dark metal surface
for ripples, disturbances across the
face of a huge lemon cheese,
pocked with delicious moulds,
that lies just under the surface.

Do I care if it's just the moon
performing a perfect charade?
Can't I already taste the acid
tang of a perfect cheese?

Somewhere, off-stage,
the foxes are laughing.

Godiva's Confession

Dear Leofric, dear lord,
I am troubled by the gossip
in the town of Coventry
that travellers are spreading.

You know my love of truth
so I must tell you that our
recent agreement, which
the townspeople speak of

was not quite as they tell it.
I did agree with you, my lord,
to ride as God made me,
upon my best loved horse,

through Coventry, and you,
my lord, agreed to waive
the hated taxes on the poor,
but there is one small thing.

The townspeople say that
Tom alone watched me
and they turned their faces
to their chamber walls;
- not quite so.

Tom, golden-haired Tom,
is blind and saw nothing,
but the townspeople kindly
cheered me on, the merchants

fairly fell from their windows,
waving their kerchiefs so fast
their wives held their legs
as I trotted by. You had said
my love of art should make
me bold for the task; it did.
and more, I have taken pity
on blind, golden-haired Tom,

who, alone, saw nothing.
He now lies by my side
seeing, exploring
the form God gave me,
- with his hands.

Your affectionate and honest wife,
Godiva.

The Virgin Mermaid
after 'Clerk Colven', 2004

...and suddenly I saw rocks
and foam thrashing,
Gulls spinning in the air,
the wind smacked my face.
So this was the land.

Creatures moved there,
their cloven tails braced,
balancing their frames
as they picked at nets.
They had no salt smell.

A boat's wake swept my back,
I rolled and saw him,
a land creature leaning down
to catch my flying arm.
He, fresh from the deep, had salt.

He lifted me from the water,
I flapped in fear and something sweeter.
He touched my scaly tail, he faltered.
We fell entangled, he struck out,
forgetting me, he sank away.

I heard the keening on the shore.
A creature wrapped in sacking
knee-deep and howling, cursed me.
So, cloven-tail her and fishy-tail me,
virgins both empty of love, locked eyes.

Allowable Mirth

Glasgow summer, pissing it down;
it's Graduation Day so reflections
in the sudden puddles on the Byres Road
show high heels, kilts and Batman robes.

This hissing temple of a bus throws water
into the path of leather-skin alkies still
dressed for that last night at The Barrows,
still dancing to stay out the rain.

In the first seat in the bus, a blind guy,
listening hard for clues, no dog, just the stick.
Outside the Metro a soaked couple push
past another blind guy, he spins into the seat

beside the first blind guy, their sticks cross and tap,
the one falls into the other, they grunt,
rearrange themselves, listening hard for clues,
'See you...' says one.
'Naw,' says the other.

Sharp as the bus décor, turquoise and purple,
quick as the flying curve of the stairs, just
for a moment they look past each other.
The passengers check for permission;
the bus shakes with allowable mirth.

Kelvingrove

We had to go – years of sighing
over illustrations in design books
made it imperative – we had to look.

Who dared say it first?
You were full of well-tutored
respect for established opinion
but you also knew the making craft,
the strength of joints, the angles
that support the human spine.

'Those chairs'- I whispered,
intimidated by the museum hush -
'they don't look very comfortable,'
thinking of those Glasgow matrons
taking tea and gossip together
in rival tea rooms, undomesticated
in fur jackets, heels and gloves,

You smiled, relishing your own
affection for a making tradition
so like your Cotswold heroes.

Never mind the Rennie-Mackintosh,
the cutlery made you weep.

Dogs Crossing The Meadows

All the long summer days,
through the ad hoc cricket games,
avoiding the dipping Frisbies,
dogs make solo dashes
across the Breughel Meadows.

Big dogs, city stifled,
quiver at 'Stay!'
Backsides trembling,
ears and tail skywards,
drinking in the acreage.

Small dogs, city flat size,
feeling a dreamed wild
radiating from their
rat-size paws, yelp in fear
and timid ecstasy.

At dusk, under orange lamplight,
Marchmont maidens and widows
converge with Westies and Yorkies
for a last feel of the fading day,
their solo tracks never touching.

All the short winter days
on snow expanses pocked
with paw marks, dogs trot,
and owners follow their tracks,
with lead, nibbles and plastic bag.

Mellis, Cheese Shop,
Victoria Street, Edinburgh

It was Edinburgh Siberia cold,
that east-born razor wind slicing,
piercing through my clothes,
and I, a Mellis virgin, that day
I entered the pungent chill cave.

Good shops are warm, welcoming,
carefully lit, loosening the purse strings
with smiles and well-informed wiles.
The space was dark, cold; the assistant
awed by her pedigreed stock, silent.

Yellow on yellow, primrose to new moon,
gorse to peace rose, orange to buttercup,
marble hard, soap soft, varicosed, aerated.
A gallery, a museum, an aromatic temple of cheese,
and I, looking for a lump of toasting cheddar.

Constitutional

November, cold afternoons on the shore,
sun gone by three from the lemon sky,
you come and find me, persuade me,
that we should walk before the dark
wipes the colour from the gorse.

Everyman and his dog are walking
the mud-squelching track, our cat
that likes to accompany us
bows out before such canine presence.
We note the small print of the weather.

On the horizontals of the water
mud and mist quiet before night,
we point, we are amazed at
the mountain's silhouette
as if it might be different from yesterday

This pattern of days, our footsteps
on the tracks and the grass,
trace more than a habit.
Our words made new each day,
in unpredictable friendship.

Hands

With wood, your hands are in control,
the push and press of the plane,
a planned path, strewing shavings,
gold ringlets tumbling,
the sweep of the saw whistling straight
through, your hand certain in the grip.
Pressing the planed wood to your lips,
your flesh detect its imperfections.

In music, your hands are dancers
sure of their allotted space,
weightless fingertips finding the note,
the chord shapes in their senses
independent of mind; then the strum,
a statement of being in the *only* place.
Holding the bow like a gift,
gifting the bow to the string.

On flesh, your hands are silent,
silky creatures exploring a world
of open aspect, mapping the paths
towards a mutual destination.
Best, in tormented moments,
your hands on my back, melting
the hard fear to liquid.

This Could Be The Last Time......

My bicycle, wrapped in a tarpaulin,
leans with yours against the shed,
Ten gears, drop handlebars,
sculpted leather saddle drying out.
A real bike, a man's bike,
a bike for Galloway's switchback
roads; tyres now sagging, like mine.

These blue sky breezy days
have you asking – what about the bikes?
But new tubes, new tyres, removing rust
lie beyond the bounds of our desire.
Let's walk instead I say to your
gentle enthusiastic face.

Don't think I don't remember
those flying moments, the hills
that rolled us down their flanks,
flies in our mouths, hair streaming,
stopping to make sweaty love
in pine forest undergrowth.

And I wonder, too,
could that last time
have been the last time
for this adventure?

And will we know,
after the fiery years of flesh,
when cooling, we shall turn
in the night
towards that glow
for the last time?

Indigo Dreams Publishing
132, Hinckley Road
Stoney Stanton
Leicestershire
LE9 4LN
www.indigodreams.co.uk